MW00333299

THE FAITH FILES

A Compilation of Testimonials

Amy L. Deanes

A Cloud of Witnesses

Superior Publishing LLC.

CONTENTS ▌

CONTENTS

CONTENTS

THIS IS FOR YOU FATHER GOD
ANOTHER CLOUD OF WITNESSES

Minister Amy L. Deanes

A GREAT CLOUD OF WITNESSES

remember growing up and listening to my Uncle, whom is a Pastor, teach bible class at my home church Palo Alto MB Church, West Point, MS. Every Wednesday night he would teach but it seemed like he always mention the great cloud of witnesses in Hebrews. These were the collection of people that God chose to brag on in Hebrews for their outstanding faith.

When I think about the great cloud of witnesses, I also think about the Hall of Fame that the world has, and also in this city that I live they also have a Hall of Fame where they induct different people from our little city to showcase. My dad even became one of the honorees in the year 2020.

But as I found my own place in the Lord, I became a witness as well. And each time I would hear or read about the great cloud of witnesses in Hebrews, I would always think, what if ....What if miraculously the Lord wanted to choose a "Cloud of Witnesses" like in the bible days to give testimony to the World that HE is STILL GOD, that He is the SAME, YESTERDAY, TODAY and FOREVERMORE!

I have thought about this for some time even to the point that I wanted to create this book, The Faith Files. I could give my testimony, but also allow other witnesses that could tell of the goodness of GOD and all that HE has done. I want to let the world know that Miracles are still being performed everyday right in front of us. Everyday when we talk to a person, we have no idea what God has done in their lives. We always talk about JESUS giving sight to the blind in the bible, but I have had the pleasure of meeting a woman named, Minister Lou Edwards Walker, a woman that can witness that she was blind, but now she's able to see. I know we know the story about the woman with the issue of blood, but I had the opportunity to witness through a Lady named Joyce Johnson's testimony that she had an issue of blood and had no blood in her body but somehow by the Grace of God she was still functioning after finding out she had cancer and how God healed her. I can go on and on about the people that shared their testimonies because GOD IS THE SAME GOD! HE is still healing the sicking. God is still being a lawyer, just like HE was for the woman that was caught in the very act of adultery, but according to the two Yolanda's in this book, he rescued them both from some harsh prison sentences that they were facing in the court room. There is NOBODY like GOD!

I have my own testimonies of how I tried God time after time. I can remember one time when I was in my early twenties, my sister and I lived together. Our phone, which then was a landline phone had been cut off for about a month. We couldn't afford to pay the bill, which was about $200 and something dollars. And me being who I was had the audacity to try God. I went and picked the phone up and it was making this loud sound, "dant, dant, dant, dant, dant, dant, dant" let's you know that it has been cut off for a while. I was frustrated and really wanted it back on. So I picked that phone up one day and I said, "Lord I know that YOU are able to turn this phone back on. I don't have the money and YOU know that I don't." I said, "Lord I'm going to check it everyday to see if you do it." And just like that everyday, I would go and pick the phone up, "dant, dant, dant, dant, dant, dant." I had gotten a little frustrated and I stopped checking it. So one day my son came running through the house and knocked the phone over and there it was, "duuuuuuunnnnnnnn" A dialtone. There was a dial tone! I grabbed that phone and put it to my ear and low and behold the phone was working! I immediately called my mom, of course and this was in the days of caller ID. When she answered I was like, "Mama! The phone is on!" And she said, "Amy where you at?" I could hear her washing dishes. I said, "I'm at home momma!" And she was like, "Ohh yall paid the bill?" I said, "No mama God did!" She laughed. I asked, "What number came up on the ID box? She said, "000000000"

That was nobody BUT GOD! The phone stayed on a good while like weeks until I wasn't satisfied with that and I called the phone company and tried to get my internet hooked back up. I kid you not, I call these people with this authority in my voice and they were trying to help me . And this lady says, "Mam what number are you calling me from?" I had no answer. Still didn't realize that I was messing up my blessing. She said, "Ma'am what number are you calling from?" I was so excited and ignorant I told her, "The Lord turned this phone on and I don't have a number." She laughed at first and she said, "Hold on! This line has been disconnected, how did you get this phone on?" I said again, "The Lord turned it on!" She asked me to hold on and a gentleman got on and asked the same question, I gave him the same answer and his come back was, "Ma'am we are going to have to turn this phone back off unless you are going to pay this bill today?" I said no sir I don't have the money to turn it back on at the time. Are you going to turn it off today?" His reply was, not today, but in about 3 days. And in exactly three days my phone was off again. But that didn't even matter, well it mattered but I had saw God's power in a CRAZY WAY!!!

After this I felt like with my FAITH I could do anything!!! And that's exactly what God wanted me to do have FAITH and know that through HIM all things were possible. And at that time in my life, they were, I was on a roll. Speaking things and watching things happen. People were coming to me to pray for them and different things. I was receiving praise reports. I was hearing from God. God was showing me miracles, signs and wonders. But I was so immature in the Word of God and in my relationship with HIM. I didn't realize what I was walking into. It was amazing! My boyfriend, at the time, which is now my husband was even amazed. Then he started coming home and telling me who to pray for at work, and even sometimes call home from work and ask me to pray for certain people while they were on the phone. God was working in and through my life.

Knowing God like that was a scary thing for me. I remember sitting in church, and He allowed me to see a person that I knew in the church sitting in front of me, get killed in a car wreck by hitting two deer. When I saw this, I was still sitting behind her and she turned and looked in my face. That scared me so bad, until I got up and left, when I got into my car and closed the door. She came out of church behind me and she was waving at me in slow motion. And then everything shattered like glass in front of me. I was so scared and nervous I could hardly get home. When I got home that stayed on my mind the entire time. When I got ready for bed, I couldn't sleep because I kept seeing the wreck. Every time I saw it, I would get down and pray and it happened twice I kept seeing it. I cried and woke my husband and told him what was going on and he kept saying it would be alright. I still couldn't sleep for seeing it.

So finally, I made him get on the floor with me to pray. We held hands and I asked him to pray for her. When he finished a calmness came over me. I was able to sleep. That next night at church, she wasn't there. And I was nervous and the members kept saying it's not like her not to be here. Testimony service begin, my uncle, Pastor Bobby made me the Mistress of Ceremony. I remember as if it was last night, that same lady came bursting into church with her hands in the air, hollering and crying, praising God. She said, "Two deer! Two deer almost killed me!" But My God blocked it!" My mouth fell open in disbelief, tears ran down my face and my heart was beating so fast I didn't know what to do." I only told a few people about the experience but I begged God to not let me ever deal with that again. It was too much for me. My Uncle told me that was my gift, it's to help others. But I was done with that I didn't want to experience that again. But what it did do, was increase my FAITH in GOD. THAT HE CAN SHOW YOU A THING, AND THEN TURN AROUND AND CHANGE IT, BECAUSE OF PRAYER and FAITH!

Ms. Montreysal Warren

THE LORD SAID, "SHIFT!"

Faith is when I can't see anything positive in my current situation but then something amazing happen!
Testimony :
For the last year in a half I had been tired of my job at the finance company.   I had been with the company a total of 12 years. I loved my job and my customer but when the pandemic was approaching

and my Vice President became the President things begin to change it like co workers had a problem with me and the boss started saying mean things and cursing at me I would just take a break go to my car and cry and pray; come back in and begin to work . Each day I would feel so unhappy and out of place. Then I would look for jobs trying to make the same thing I was making there until one Sunday at church a guy got up told his testimony about when He renew his YES to God and he resign from playing the drums at church and begin to service our Pastor and God open doors for him. He said he felt he was in the way of others elevation because things got better for him as people he was connected to. So at the end of May my boss curse me out for closing out before 5:30 which message and said we can close at 5:30. So he said get my things and get out his office which this is the clean Version. Then he had the supervisor to call and said I was suspended with no pay and I just left the key I didn't go back. I was out of work for two months received a job not even making half of what I use to but I am at peace and I'm so much happier. I got behind on my house and when they call for the payment they said I had to the 25th of October to pay $3700. Coming up to the due date I receive a text from my Pastor who didn't know what was going on but gave me a word. The next day I receive a message from my sister in Christ she said read 2 King 7 chapter and she sent me a prayer. I had also watch a TikTok and the guy said read the month you was born the chapter in each book of the Bible and the verse of your birthday. In my morngin prayer I would say, " Lord I trust you and I know you going to do it for me and my girls."   So Saturday before the 25th I told my friend Tykia what was going on and she said don't go off of the natural due date go off the spiritual one. And that Monday she sent me a prayer and she and her church sowed a seed in my life, after I received it, I went to Genesis 12:3 ERV "I will bless those who bless you, and I will curse those who curse you. I will use you to bless all the people on earth.""

I sent it to my friend after I read it. So my house people call while I was at work but I couldn't answer at the time. So when I got home I call back and the lady said hold on.   I was nervous but never lose faith she came back she said Mrs Warren we was just calling to say we can give you a six month extension and if you get some money just set it to the side until the six month is up. I begin to praise God! As I was speaking in tongues, I heard God say, "Shift!"
So in this season of my life I'm learning to shift. I know where I am isn't all it's going to be for me. In Jesus Name

Montresyal

Mrs. Bonnie Perry

IT'S GOT TO BE A GOD SOMEWHERE

In 1997 I was coming home from work just thinking how good God is even the little things and it came to me IT GOT TO BE A GOD SOME WHERE!! And verses started flowing in my heart that's when I wrote the song. In 2012 I lost my son and almost lost my mine! My HEART was broken into pieces I did think it would ever mend back together, But God !! I couldn't wait until everybody leave home in the morning so I could scream and cry my heart out!! A voice came to me and said "Moma! Why are you crying so hard do you know who I'm with? I'm with JESUS!" God kept me y'all. Im not saying I don't still hurt and miss him! I'm saying God calm the storm!! YES IT GOT TO BE A GOD SOME WHERE!! He walked with me every step of the way!! I have the right to praise him!! Who wouldn't serve a God like this!

It's deep when you lose a child, I would tell them without God ain't no way you can make it. You have to trust him with all your might and believe that he can fix anything even a broken heart if he bring you to it he will take you through it

Bonnie Perry

Mrs. Gaylor Wofford

I DIDN'T KNOW I WAS IN THE WORLD

The lord has been good to me. I was in a bad car accident in 2005. I broke my neck, my arm, fractured my ribs and my pelvic bone. I didn't know I was in this world and all of my kids and my niece were with me. My kids were only scratched up. My niece had a rod put in her leg, but I Thank God we didn't lose our lives.

Mrs. Lamonica Calvert

I WAS DETERMINED TO WALK AGAIN

In June of 1996, I was in a car accident on highway 47(Trebloc/west point area). I was traveling home with my 11 month old baby girl named Alexus and my 3 year old bonus son Trey. When I approached the curve on 47, I saw an 18 wheeler and thought he saw me. Apparently he didn't and he hit me head on. I never lost conscious. I could feel and see the motor on my legs. Sawana Walker and Tater Rowe arrived on the scene and were able to get my children out the car. The driver of the 18 wheeler broke the back window out my car and was able to pull me out through the back because my door was jammed and wouldn't open. After having surgery, I was told that I would never be able to wear regular shoes again. I would have to have special made shoes. I messed my legs up bad. I have a plate on my right leg from my knee all the way down my leg. My left foot was crushed to the bones and had three pins put in it. I laid flat on my back for a year and had to learn how to walk all over again. During this time, my husband had to move me back into my parent's home because he couldn't take care of me due to the fact he worked in Tupelo.

It took a little over a year for me to learn how to walk again. Yes, I had doubts because I was used to wearing heels all the time. I never bought gym shoes and knowing that I might not ever be able to wear heels again or maybe not walk. But my God said no! I will never leave nor forsake you my child. I thank Him that He saw fit in little ole me to give me another chance to wear heels and walk. As of today, when I stand for long hours at work, my ankles will swell but that's alright because I got legs and I can walk! I got a mouth and I can talk and tell a dying world of the goodness of our Lord and Savior Jesus Christ!!!!!

I was determined to walk again and now I am and I thank and praise God for showing me favor and mercy!

Lamonica Calvert

My Grandchildren, My Motivation
Author Jacqueline Allen

MY FOOD HAD GOTTEN
REALLY LOW

Since 2014 it has been a struggle for me trying to survive for me and the twins. They cut my check off. Then for 3 months they gave me $19.00. Then they cut off again. Then after about 3 months they finally gave me $69.00 for a few months, then they raised it up to $350.00 for about a year. I have been living off $614.00 up until about 6 months ago. I got a letter Monday telling me in December I will start getting my full benefits. I don't know how I would have made it had it not been for my faith in God. Every time I received a blessing God told me who to bless. I was like Lord if I do that how am I going to pay my bills He said trust me my child. I have never once had to be in the dark, never once was we without water. My food got real low and I drink coffee all day so there would be enough to feed the kids. I did not complain I trusted God that He would provide. He never came when I wanted him to but He always showed up on time. I learned to be content in any situation. I know it was God.

SECOND TESTIMONY:

The doctor told me today that I got to learn to live with the pain. This is my testimony for the past 5 years I have been dealing with a pain from a injury that happened over 20 years ago. I have had 3 surgeries. For the past 5 years I have been in a boot or a cast starting at the beginning of fall and lasting until the first of spring. Glory to God I lived with the pain no pain medication just Jesus and me. So I really understood what the doctor was saying. Living with the pain has allowed me to write and publish a book called Through the pain and another book ◈ called starting over new that's soon to come out. Living with the pain has allowed me a family that has loved me, prayed for me but most of all that allowed me to be me while God was working on me to become who he wants me to be. He works on me all the time but during the fall I got to fall back because he found something else that he wants to fix on and then in the spring I spring up and do what he's taught me in my life during the time my faith I mean my faith in the night season was being put to the tested. By the Glory of God I have lived with the pain no pain medication just Jesus and me. So now I don't know where this part of my journey is going to lead me but to Jesus I am a living testimony that Jesus will never leave you or forsake you but He will do JUST WHAT HE SAID HE WILL DO

Jackie

I FELT WEAK AT TIMES...

First of all I would love to Thank God. As 2020 we went through a bad situation with my daughter being 5 months pregnant and she got COVID. The beginning of the year 2021. My daddy got COVID on January of 2021. My son got diagnosed with Testicular Cancer in March of 2021. He had 2 surgery and he had to take chemotherapy from May 3rd - June of 21. In the month of June my grandson was diagnosed with RSV he was put into the hospital. Therefore at the time my so and grandson both was going through it. I didn't know what to do at first but God step in right on time. In November 3rd 2021. We went to his 6 weeks check up and his doctor came in and said that everything was looking good. I wanted to jump up and do a hallelujah dance in that doctor office. I'm here to tell you that God is soooo good. I give him all the prayers. I felt weak at times but I made a promise to my mother before she died that I would never let my kids, my daddy ever see me break down I have been doing just what she asked me to do. She also told me to keep looking to the hill where all my help come from.

Barabara Powell

Mrs. Barbara Powell

WHEN I FOUND THE TRUE LOVE OF GOD

He's done a Wonderful thing for me

Mrs. Tammy West

I honestly can't say that I've always had faith. But I always knew. And there were circumstances where I just had survival skills whenever my situation was hard for me. I didn't just consciously have faith that things are going to happen or things were going to go this way when it was supposed to go quite the opposite when I was in the world.

I thank God for building my faith, from situation to situation. My childhood, from being sexually abused, my drug addiction, and living a gay lifestyle. I've been through a lot! One was depression, I have mental issues but I think my battle is my real faith. It was built coming on this side. This side is learning how to live through it all. He's brought me through so much from my childhood up until I walked into Holy Ghost Temple. And I was still fighting with some issues, but my faith has increase due to trials tribulations, counseling from my pastor, and going through many storms.   I've learned the game. The faith I have now is my insightful wisdom of what true faith is growing up. I'm very trusting and naive. And I think that came from watching television shows and my idea of being so optimistic as one of the see people. I wanted to see Him, believing in people and wanted to believe that they were more than probably they were really showing. That was my mistake, I got in a lot of trouble throughout my life now.   I'm not going to say that I was a victim because it was a lot of de- cisions I made. I'm not going to throw anybody under the bus because truly I made my own mis- takes and my own decisions.   I'm not going to even blame it on my being naive, because I still made those decisions I made those decisions to pick up that to pick up those drugs I made the decision start dating women even though the thing the circum- stances surrounding those factors was a lot of anger a lot of rage feeling left out wanting to be loved anger and all of the above.

I just wanted to believe. I put too much faith in people, more than I did in myself or even God. Even now it's God, because the fact it was even different because of the way I was brought up as a child which is another story for another time but as I grew to know for myself who God truly was I guess it was more than just existing.

Sometimes I didn't even feel real or like a person sometimes. Picture this, like I was just walking around like in the real world always thinking about being in my own head. But when I found out the true love of God and I had a purpose in my life I realize if I did have a purpose now I'm not saying I knew what there purpose was instantly but I knew I had a purpose at least for the most part I begin to feel like my existence had a purpose and I wasn't just subhuman that I wasn't just walking around here existing.

I have so much pain in my life few attempts on suicide and thoughts of suicide especially, when I was on drugs.   I was always thinking about committing suicide.   I just felt so hopeless so lost walking around here in this world where do I fit in?   Why was I even born with something that always came along in my head why did my parents even have me?   But like I said from the former statements up until when I got saved, I realize that all was not lost.   I got married to a man that loves me dearly and cherishes me.   I have family and friends and I truly feel loved now.   For a long time you couldn't tell me that that I was loved or worth loving.   You couldn't make me believe that but because of the love of God, I know that He's truly real. It would take me a million lifetimes and 5000 pages or more to really tell you my story.   But this is my testimony, God's love is real and he loves us so much.   You'll never be outta place or out of reach with Him.   I was never too far gone.   I love Him so much! Today I can identify with Mary Magdalene, because I had so many afflictions but he delivered me out of them all.   If somehow I could imagine myself sitting somewhere alone with Him, looking into His eyes with so much compassion smiling at me, after He delivered me out of all those demons! Yes, I feel like Mary Magdalene.

Just a touch from Him and I was never the same. Even though there were many attempt as he tried to call on me, I went back, but I'm glad I finally made the decision to give my life toHim.   This is a decision I'm never ever ever ever going to regret!   I might regret the things I did in my youth BUT GOD at 52 , yes I got saved!   It's never too late and I'm grateful.   I might regret a lot of things but being saved will never be one of them.

AMY L. DEANES

TAMMY WEST

Dr. Shelia Evans

THERE IS NO WAY I WOULD HAVE SURVIVED IN MY OWN STRENGTH

What built my faith?

Life has been my Faith builder for as long as I can remember through the seen and unseen. Through the good, bad and ugly.

First, I'll deal with the a little bit of unseen, bad and ugly. As a child when I thought I was all alone. I would look around and see no one. When I was being touched in areas that a child should not have been touched. When I cry for help and saw no visible person to aid me. When I was hungry or scared or wished life was no more. When I was mad, angry, sad and didn't know love, couldn't recognize love nor did I know how to receive love because love was never shown to me.

All the time I thought I was alone but their was a what I thought to be an invisible GOD WHO was their all the times. I know that now because there is no way I would have survived in my own strength. All the time I was operating in a strength not my own. Hallelujah ◇◇◇◇◇◇◇◇◇◇.

Hebrew 11: 1 states, Now faith is the substance of things hoped for, the evidence of things not seen. There were a lot of NOW moments in my life and I continue to experience them today.

Through life journey of many many mistakes, traveling down the wrong road and bumping my head I began to recognize GODS hand in my life. I began to see God at work in my life. God was visible in my life. He began turning my misery into my messages. He showed me Himself in all my heartaches and pains. He showed that it was HE WHO was cradling me, holding me, showing me the way out all the time. Psalm 32:8 states, I will instruct thee and teach thee in the way which thou shalt go: I will guide thee with mine eye.

I learned that although I endured much I'm not defined by what I endured. He showed me that I'm the apple ◇ of His eye. I'm fearfully and wonderfully made. No good thing will He with hold from me. 3 John 2 states, Beloved, I wish above all things that thou mayest prosper and be in health, even as thy soul prospereth. Glory to GOD◇◇◇◇.

Why is Faith important.

Because Hebrew 12:6 states, But without faith it is impossible to please him: for he that cometh to God must believe that he is, and that he is a rewarder of them that diligently seek him.

Mark 11:23 states, For verily I say unto you, That whosoever shall say unto this mountain, Be thou removed, and be thou cast into the sea; and shall not doubt in his heart, but shall believe that those things which he saith shall come to pass; he shall have whatsoever he saith.

God has proven Himself to be faithful to me over and over again. Therefore it is imperative for me to please Him and it is only through faith that I can please God. God is the reason I breathe for I live and have my being in him. Without Him I am nothing. God brought me and is keeping me where I am today. I LOVE GOD! Blessings ◇◇◇◇

Dr. Shelia R. Evans
(662) 617-4759
Psalm 138:8 The LORD will perfect that thing which concerneth me.

The daughters that I lost.

IT TOOK ME A LONG TIME...

When you have faith God will allow you to see things no one can see .. Like an imagine of a loved one that has past on are a dream of that person that is now with our God. When you have faith God will make things clear in your mind and heart like a test that you have tried to take three times and felled . After the second time you probably lost your faith but with God the third time you past ... Faith and God go hand and hand with one you don't have the other. I do believe that God can sometimes put you in a position just so he can show you who he is . When you have Gods faith he opens doors and keep them open until you get that this door is meant for you to walk through and receive what God has for you ... I lost the faith after I lost my girls and i know I'm a work in progress .It took me a long time but I do believe that God has a plan for and a purpose . And yes I do have faith now .. God is so awesome thank You!

The daughter I gained.

And now I have a lil girl that's three and a grand daughter that's eight . They keep me busy but its worth it ..
Wiley Deanes

My grandaughter

I HAD A BIOPSY AND IT CAME BACK CANCER

First I give all thanks to my Lord and Savior for His grace & mercy is what has bought me this for and to my prayer warriors thank you for your prayers. I had said I wasn't going to tell what was going on with me but God won't let me keep my mouth close, two weeks ago I had a biopsy and it came back cancer and you know how I was feeling but I am human. My children, grandchildren, and sisters and brothers, & friends were right by my side but I know a man that sticks closer than any brother, on yesterday I went in the hospital and the tumor was removed from my kidneys.

When I say He is an Awesome Grateful & Merciful God Yessssss He is if you going through something no matter what it is give it to Him and I guarantee He will fix it for you!!!

I'm doing good in just a little pain and a little sore had a restless night but I'm still here I just had give my testimony!!! God is good y'all and I Love him because he first loved me he has been so so good I cannot tell it all. You all have a Blessed and great day and I Love y'all and y'all can't do a thing about it I am a living testimony all praises unto Him prayers work y'all!!!!

HE KEEPS ON MAKING A Way for me!

Ms. Dorothy Hubbard

Another Testimony: In 2014 I was at my doctors office and my heart rate was dropping the nurse kept coming back checking me my doctor finally came in after she told him something was wrong he checked me again and decided I needed to be ambulance to Tupelo hospital my heart rate had dropped under 30 but God held me until we arrived in Tupelo hospital and kept me safe all that night and the next day I received a pacemaker in my chest Thank you God for keeping me Hallelujah Yessssss God is real!! Dorothy Hubbard

Bishop & Pastor Dowdell

MY MOM AND HUSBAND BOTH WERE DEALING WITH HEART ISSUES

I wanted to send you a testimony that is dear to my heart in relation to my husband and mother being sick at the same time about 2 years ago they both had a issue with their hearts where my mom had a light heart attack and a stroke they were looking for her to have a small percentage to survive after 7 stents but she is healed today as we all made much prayer to God she came from rehabilitation to home doing she was doing at first to God be the glory and my husband the doctors said he was fighting for his life due to heart issues but we all begin to petition God for his healing after much prayer, faith and trusting God almighty God allowed him to overcome He is healed today! Thank you Jesus!! God is still a miracle worker and healer!!!

Thank you for allowing me to share these testimonies with you!

Pastor Joyce Dowdell

Minister Shonda Deloach

THE WEEK OF MY FATHER'S DEATH

The dictionary defines grief as deep sorrow, especially that caused by someone's death. In other words, its, sorrow, misery, sadness, pain, distress, agony, heartbreak, broken-heartedness, affliction and the list go on.

After the death of my father in 2011, I begin to experience depression. Even though my father wasn't in my life growing up, when he did decide to return home, after sometime, I begin to feel like a little girl all over again.

The week of my father's death, that is when my family and I learned he had lung cancer, and it had spread over the majority of his body. The doctor's told us there was nothing more they could do for him but to send him home on Hospice and let time run its course. That Wednesday morning, I was sitting with him, he wasn't eating, he had stopped eating, but this particular morning, he wanted ice cream. I ran to the nurse's station telling them he wants ice cream; the nurse gave me the ice cream and I went back to his room as fast as I could. I begin to give him the ice cream little by little, Praise God, he ate it all. I was so happy, was starting to want food, yes if he eats, he will get his strength, I thought. When I sat down, my father jumped in the bed, I asked him what was wrong and he told me a man was standing by the door, and as long as I was with him, the man wasn't going to get him. I reassured him that no one was in the room, but he insisted that it was.

Thursday came and it was time to go home, my husband had gone and moved the bed out so they could get the hospital bed and other equipment that was needed in the room. The ambulance brought him home got him set up and they left, the Hospice nurse was there to make sure he was connected to his oxygen and that it was flowing from the pump through his nose. Once she got that situated, she told us they would be back in the morning and she left. I stayed for a few more minutes to make sure he was doing ok, I told my mom that I would be back, tomorrow which was that Friday, after I got off work, I told my dad I loved him, I would see him tomorrow and I left.

Friday morning while working, I received a call from my mom letting me know my dad had an accident and the nurses hadn't made it yet, I told her I would be there shortly. Once I arrived, I got him all cleaned up, I told him I loved him and I would see him at 3 when I got off. When I got back to work, before I could sit down, my phone ranged again, this time, they were letting me know my father was gone. How could he, I had just left him.

After everything was over, the funeral, my family and friends had left, returning back to their destinations, I was finally able to lay down and try to get some much needed rest. Once I closed my eyes, thy flew open, all I could hear in my ear was "you left him and the man got him". I started screaming and crying, my husband came in the room asking what was the matter, I told him, "That man got my dad". I knew better, I knew the will of the Lord was going to be done, but the enemy began to play tricks with my mind, all I could think about was "I left him". Depression had found my address and it looked like she was going to staying a while. I didn't want to go to work, I didn't want to participate in anything, I would go to church and just sit there, I would eat here and there, sitting in the house with all of the lights off. I went to the doctor, she told me she would try me on some anti-depressants, which made my situation worse, how could something designed to help me, make me feel worse than I already did?

There is no way I could go on like this, my mom would talk to me, my family, my pastor, and even my friends would stop by to try and get me out of the house, I could not shake it, "I left him and the man got him". All I would do is cry, I beat myself up so badly, I begin to lose weight, I was slowly slipping in a place, where if God didn't come and rescue me, then it wouldn't get done. I didn't have the strength to pull my own self out, the more people tried to talk me out of it, the deeper I got.

I had a doctor's appointment, a follow up, she wanted to see how I was adjusting to the medication. Once she walked in the room, I guess she could tell I wasn't doing good. She asked me how was I doing on the medication, I looked at her and shook my head, letting her know I wasn't doing, I had stopped taking it because I didn't like how it made me feel. She asked me was I shaking my head replying no to her question or no the medication isn't working? I told her, "I was shaking my head because I was letting you know, no I wasn't taking it anymore". She told me that was the worst thing I could have done to just stop taking and without directions on how to wean myself off of it. At that point I didn't even care, my father left me and it was all my fault. She looked at me and she said, "Mrs. DeLoach, you are going to have to come out of this, I can send you somewhere where you can rest", I looked up at her and said "so you are suggesting WillowBrook"? She said, it will help you to rest, get you back on your feet so you can return to your normal life. With tears rolling down my face, I looked at and I told her, "I will not go out like this", something had awakened inside of me, my will to live had changed, I knew it was going to be a long road ahead, but with God on my side, I was ready for the journey.

When I left that office, I went home and I feel down on my knees, first asking God for forgiveness, because I knew the Will of the Lord was going to be done whether I accepted it or not. I knew there wasn't a man in my father's room, I seen it for myself. I asked God to take control of my life and with His help, I was going to be victorious. In time, God begin to heal my hurt, lift my head, gave me my smile back, put joy back in my heart. I would quote scriptures that pertained to my situation, "Lord by Your stripes, I am healed, "you will keep me in perfect peace if I keep my mind on You", and my favorite, "Now unto Him who is able to do exceeding, abundantly above all I could ask or think, but it is according to the power that worketh in us, I made it personal by saying me".

I read a quote and it said, "Grief never ends. But it changes. It's a passage, not a place to stay. Grief is not a sign of weakness, nor is it a lack of faith. It is the price of love". -author unknown-

Grief is a real emotion, and it's one of the most common experienced emotions by humans. Grief doesn't mean you are weak nor does it mean you don't have the faith, grief is a natural reaction to any type of loss, whether it is the loss of a loved one, the ending of a relationship, loss of a job, or whatever the loss maybe.

Grief teaches us about faith, it teaches us patience, grief teaches us not to take our loved ones for granted, it teaches us to be true to ourselves and it teaches us that its ok to grieve.

So, my brothers and sisters, if you find yourself in a place of grief, look to the hills from whence comes your help, all your help comes from the Lord. God sees He knows and He cares.

Matthew 11:28-30 reads, "come to me, all you who are weary and burdened, and I will give you rest. Take my yoke upon me and **learn from me**, for I am gentle and humble in heart, and you will find rest for your souls. For **MY** yoke is easy and my burden is light.

Evangelist Shonda Deloach

Pastor Cheryl Hych

I WAS DIAGNOSED WITH RHEUMATIC FEVER

Unconscious Faith

In the year of 1965 at the age of 6, I was diagnosed with Rheumatic Fever.

I remember arriving one Sunday at a local church for service and could not move my legs. My parents took me to the doctor and was told that I had this disease that affects the heart with murmurs. They were given a food list of things that I needed to eat in moderation plus l was limited to a lot of activities that a child would normally do. If these things were not controlled it would result in rapid heart beats

At certain times being unable to walk would flair up.

I was in and out of school from the 1st grade until the 6th grade. I remember my parents carrying me from the bed to the couch during these times. My teachers would make sure they bring my homework to me (this was before integration). I was taking shots monthly from the local Health Department. Since it was close to the school I would walk to have these administered.

One day while going to this appointment, I decided I'm tired of being stuck in the hip and having a knot and soreness for two or three days. My mind was made up that I'm not taking these shots the rest of my life. So I stopped taking them without telling my parents.

Later I realized that was my beginning of walking by Faith!!

I was unconsciously led to TRUST GOD.

Every checkup from then to now has been negative for heart murmurs.

Lord I thank you for that child like FAITH decision.

Because of that many trials and tribulations that I have experienced have been defeated because you taught me early to use the God kind of Faith!!

Pastor Cheryl Hych
TUPELO, MS

I BEGIN TO HALLUCINATE SEEING PEOPLE THAT WERE ALREADY DEAD!

Mrs. Tonia Patterson

So thankful. Health and strength is a true blessing from God. So thankful that God allowed my family and I to defeated this COVID-19 that attacked our bodies. It wasn't easy at all but we had to fight. I was so sick but God let me knew He was with us even though some days i didn't have the strength to talk to Him when I have a talk with Him everyday but the words"Lord Have Mercy". I also want to say thanks to our family and friends for everything. Love you all. A relationship and knowing who Jesus is our Lord and Savior makes a difference.

#wouldnothavedefeatedcovid19with-outJesus

I need to add how Satan tried to make me afraid thinking about death as a healthcare working I was seeing what covid was during to others and fear began to grip me! The isolation people looked at you some kind of way if you were diagnosed with COVID. I knew I had COVID on the first symptom I experienced I found the strength to get up and the first thing I saw was the mirror in my bathroom and the Holy Spirit dropped 2Timothy 1:7 in my mind. Me and my husband never prayed together been married for 26 years I always pray for him but not with him. But God keep speaking to me to get up out that bed and pray with your husband. I had no strength nor did he. We had shortage of breath fever that wouldn't break but I knew I had to be obedient to God word. I was told if I didn't get up move Around I was gonna end up in hospital on ventilator but I trusted God and believed in the faith of God. COVID attacked my body and my mind. I began to hallucinate seeing people that were already dead! I thank God for His healing just so much thankfulness I can't type it all.

TONIA THOMPSON PATTERSON

Minister Clea Cousins

AND ONE DAY, IT JUST HAPPENED

It was Spring 2021, I went to Philadephia, PA to visit my sister-in-law that was pretty sick. I stayed with my other sister-in-law, and she had an upstairs. I had no problems getting up and down the stairs everyday. But this one particular day I came down and I slipped and fell. I came tumbling down six steps and I couldn't get up. I just lye there, trying to figure out what happened. I didn't have anything on my mind that I can remember. I was paying attention. But I couldn't figure out what had happened.

I called my husband to come and help me, because I was unable to get up. He and another family member came and they got me up. The fall was bad enough that I had to be taken to the hospital.

Seeing the doctor, it seemed things were really bad. He expressed that he could see the opening of the wound...but because of the way it was there was no way to sew it or really do anything to it. He advised me that once I got back to Mississippi to keep a watch on it and see my regular doctor.

I went to see my Doctor, and the same thing, she didn't know what to do about it, she even asked me what did they want her to do to it. I had no answers. So she sent me to wound care, every time I went to wound care and go to see my Doctor she would say it's not looking any better. It looks like it's getting worse. They didn't know what to do, but I did. I kept on praying and I kept on believing, I had no choice. The doctor kept sending me to different places instead of waiting and trying. But I kept on believing.

ONE DAY, IT JUST HAPPENED....I was healed. I was healed so good, I didn't even have a limp. NEVER give up on God. Just know that it will happen one day.

I AM WALKING JUST FINE!! GLORY BE TO GOD!

Minister Clea Cousins

Mrs. Carmilla Harrison

YES IT'S CANCER

Give God all the glory. Back in Oct 2018 I was working in a place I grew to love. I loaded my machine sat back and waited on the machine to weld the part. I then folded my arms laid my hand on my left breast an felt a knot. I didn't panic but I got a little worried, like what is this? I went to the line an told my oldest daughter, Kiara, to come to the rest room with me. And to make a long story short, I went to my surgeon and he did all the test and it came back cancer. My husband Vernon and my baby girl were at the doctor office with me, when he tells me, " Yes it's Cancer." I went into hospital on Nov 2018 to get the breast removed. I started chemo in Dec of 2018. I took 16 treatment of chemo 30 straight days of radiation.

The radiation was the worst anyone could ever take. But with God's help I made it. I've been cancer free for 2 years and I am still here.

It's 2021 I have good days as well as bad days, but I am still here and going to keep fighting everyday with God's help.

I LOST EVERYTHING

In 2017, I lost everything and when I say everything I truly mean everything. My house, my furniture, my vehicle, and ultimately my job. Everything I felt was important and I had prayed so very hard to have. It started in August of 2016, when I was first diagnosed with diabetes. The medication I was placed on broke me down to where I could barely function or get out of the bed. I was unable to work and steadily began to get behind on bills. The worst part was how the people assisting me with my payments were suddenly denying me with barely any time consideration to due dates. I began applying for loans after loans in an attempt to make payments, but eventually that was becoming harder to do. I prayed and prayed for The Lord to help me so that I would keep what I had. Each time, I heard nothing and slowly depression was reintroducing itself to my life. My landlord was a wonderful person and attempted to help me as much as he could. I was grateful for everything he did, but soon came to realize that even his small gestures were simply not enough. On June 1, 2017 I moved out of my home and it felt as if I left myself at that time. Everything within me shut down like a life support machine that had received its instruction that it was time to let go to move to the next person. I moved in with my eldest daughter and my one year old grandchild. Sharing a two bedroom apartment with one of the children I had raised to go out and live life to the fullest. I remember thinking how did this happen? How did I get to this point again? Why am I revisiting a period I had seen so many times before? I thought about what people would say and how people would laugh. I considered what many had said about me in my past and slowly began to think it was true. I was so ashamed of how far I fell and how I had to depend on my child to give me a place to stay. I was homeless, broke, and everything I had was packed up in a storage. I did not want anyone to know how far I fell and had no desire to leave the house. One night, my strength was all but gone and a wailing was rising up within me that I could not contain. I believe my daughter felt my spirit because suddenly she asked if I wanted something from one of the restaurants prompting me to say "Yes". As soon as she walked out the door with my grandchild, I dropped to my knees and cried out to The Lord. My first cry was "Why, Lord, why did you allow this to happen to me? Have I not suffered enough?" Immediately The Lord answered me. Speaking as clearly as these words I am typing. He said, "I gave you what you desired, but never once did you ask Me whether it was what I desired for you." At that moment I dropped my head and wepted. He said, "Now can you trust me to give you what I desired for all to know and see that it was I who gave it to you? Can you serve me and believe me?" My response to Him, "yes, Lord, I can." Four years later, and serving The Almighty during that time, I have my new home that He desired to give me. Yet believing Him for the greater. Faith comes by hearing and hearing by the word of God. Even in loss, He is worth trusting. Trust the process. God bless.

Prophetess Nekeshia Gibson

Prophetess Nekeshia Gibson

THE JAWS OF LIFE HAD TO CUT ME OUT

Minister Melissa Hamlett

My Testimony

In the year of 1996 I was on my way to work. I was coming from highway 32 headed into town. During this time there were traffic lights and no four way stops. My light turned green and I proceeded to go forth when all of a sudden "Bam"! I was hit by an eighteen wheeler headed south. The impact was so hard that it knocked me on the parking lot that is now known as Food Giant. Sunflower was the grocery store back then and they had gas pumps on the parking lot. When my car landed on the parking lot, spectators say I was only a couple of inches from hitting them. The Jaws of life had to be called to cut me out the car. I was trapped! My mind, even at this time can remember only bits and pieces of the initial ordeal.

I remember being in the hospital and my body was in so much pain. I had broken ribs, slipped disks, broken fingers, and a hematoma in the front of my head the size of a baseball. Everyone that came to see me kept telling me I was blessed to be alive. At the time it wasn't really registering to me just how bad the accident was.

After my release from the hospital, I was at home trying to regain my strength while I visited several different doctors to get me back on track. One day after coming back from therapy, I asked my mother to take me where my car was located so I could see it. She hesitated for a moment but then she agreed to take me to the junk yard where it was located. The minute I laid eyes on the car, my heart sank. I then understood why so many people were saying I was blessed to be alive. As I stood looking at the car that looked like a smashed up can, I realized that God had kept me covered from death. Yes I was broken in places with bruises and scars but I was "Alive"!. I think this was the first time I actually realized just how powerful the merciful hand of God is. I'm alive today because of His grace. It wasn't my time. God has work for me to do. It was eleven years later that God called me into the ministry. In 1996 things weren't so clear to me but when He called my name, I understood why death was cancelled for me in that car accident. I still thank and praise God for His protection and love. This is just one of the many many things God has done in my life. I'm honored to share His graciousness with others.

MELISSA HAMLETT

I DIED AND SAW MY GRANDMA AND MOMMA

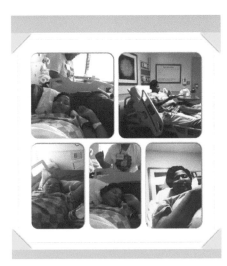

Mrs. Cassandra Davidson

November 2013 changed my life completely. I got sick and went to the doctor. He said I had bronchitis and gave me medicine and a shot. That didn't help me, I got worse. I could not eat, I had no energy, I had fever that wouldn't break, and all I wanted to do is sleep. So a couple days later, I got worse. I called my aunt over to help me get cleaned up because I could barely breathe. We called the ambulance and come to find out I ended up with pneumonia in my left lung .

I got admitted to Houston hospital on a Wednesday, while I was there I was getting treated but that Saturday night before day, it felt like an elephant was sitting on my chest. I could not breathe. My oxygen level had went to 75 percent so my nurse called the ER doctor to notify him about my situation. He told him to give me breathing treatments, but that didn't help, so he said to get her out of here now. They called a helicopter, I had to be flown to ICU, he said I would have not made in by ambulance.

I went to the unit, after being there for 2 days, the doctor informed me that he needed to sedate me to let my lungs rest because I had double pneumonia. So I told him to call my dad and husband and tell them. I told him to do everything he had to do to make me better. After being sedated, I turned for the worse my kidneys begin to fail and my family was called in numerous times.

Doctors were saying there isn't anything they can do for me but God. I had some prayers sent up . I died! I saw my grandma and mom they told me to go back. After being sedated for about 2 to weeks, I was awaken. I didn't know how I got there, who I was, and what was going on. I stayed on dialysis like 2 weeks, my kidney started functioning properly. Glory to God. I have some awesome people in my life who helped me learn me again. When I learned how to again I was excited and I used the bathroom with a diaper on!

God is awesome I'm so forever grateful for HIM keeping me alive. Isaiah 53:5... NO MATTER WHAT IT LOOKS LIKE KEEP THE FAITH AND KEEP ON BELIEVE GOD WILL SEE YOU THROUGH. I DON'T LOOK LIKE WHAT I BEEN THROUGH I AM A LIVING TESTIMONY!!

I WENT INTO THE COURTROOM, BUT DIDN'T SEE THE JURY

Yolanda Robinson

LET ME START OFF BY SAYING GIVING HONOR TO GOD WHO'S THE HEAD OF MY LIFE . I WANTED TO OPEN UP AND SHARE A TESTIMONY OR TESTIMONIES WITH YOU .

In 2003 I went through one the worst experiences in my life of living . I was in a domestic situation with a ex. We got into a serious altercation that almost cause me penitentiary time ,and I almost took his life . This is something I had to go through to get to . Let me share my story . A lot of women are involved in domestic disputes,and they are afraid to speak out . I was a victim of that . I didn't know the system was set up like it was during that time . Instead of me getting help letting the system know that I was in a abusive relationship I took matters into my own had . After fighting with him a weapon ended up being involved that could have killed him . Instead going through months and months of waiting until trail I didn't know who GOD was I heard about a man name Jesus and the fact he was the Son of God coming up in church . While going through . I will never forget God sent a sweet angel to me and the lady said . I don't know what you are going through ,but God told me to tell you that your case is already worked out . God said just praise him before the hearing. I didn't know how to praise God . One day I was sitting in the room and tears began to roll out my eyes because I never been in trouble with the law .As tears was rolling, words came out I never knew would , my feet started moving ,my hands went up . I felt something I never felt in my life . A week after that . I went to court to hear the judge say the parents left a note on there behalf . My heart dropped,but I kept hearing the angel voice saying it's already worked out . I went into the courtroom, I didn't see a jury it was only me ,the judge ,clerk,security,the officers that pick me up , and the district attorney. I looked I said court suppose to be full of people I thought . When I sitting there a angel appeared and said i know there is still some fear in you , but do not fear for my father is with you . By that time the D.A called me to the back. Remind you no jury or nothing . The D.A and I went in a small room and he asked me . Have you ever played baseball. I said when I was younger . He said I can tell from the distance the weapon was thrown to were the victim was he smiled about my body strength. He also said . The parents of the man said you told them that there son was abusing you , So ! Wtbs you never been in any trouble, and the parents want you to have your freedom ,Instead of giving you 10yrs behind bars we gone give you 5yrs on probation. My God ,My God . I still feel a praise inside of me . I walked away with my life . I'm living to live again , I walked away with my freedom , I was able to go home to my family and my babies , To God be the Glory . I wanna encourage all ladies . Get help ! If you are in domestic relationships . Get help before it's to late. This was a blessing to come out ,and a lesson to never allow the hands of the enemy to come upon me again . There is nothing or nobody in this life worth you loosing your soul over ,or serving time for . It's real . Get out and get help . I had to loose a lot just to gain what God have for me . I lost to gain wisdom and a closer walk with a man I didn't know back then, but My God I knew him on a personal level that day in that court room . God I thank you for your angels ,I thank you for being God . I know a lawyer that never lost a case . I was always told by Gods mouthpieces that my faith in God will make mountains move . I have so much faith in him . But, we all know God will test that faith.

I'm 2019 I was working a job in Columbus. I'm not shame to tell this story . I went to work with 3.00 that morning . When I got off I was hungry . There was a Burger King across the street from the job . I went over to get me something to eat . I was saying to myself . I don't have enough to buy me a meal . I ordered from the 1.00 menu . I couldn't here what my total was . As I was moving up to get my total there was a grey van in front of me with a handicap tag . As I was getting closer to pay . I kept saying . Let me get out this line I'm shame I don't have enough . I heard the voice of God saying turn that wheel back in drive-thru . I said but I don't have enough . After doing that about 3 times and God fussing at me every time I tried to turn out to leave 😊 I finally made it to the window to pay . The lady at window handed me out my receipt. I never had this to happen now . I said ma'am I didn't pay for my food . She said I know the lady in the grey van did . I pulled up rolled my window down and said thank you so much . I said that to say this . While I was trying to figure it out, God had already worked it out . My God,My God . Faith without work is dead . God tested my level of faith that day . Now when I'm in stores blessing others . It feel good to say . Can I pay for your items . Thank you God . See sometimes we don't know God already have a angel or angels on standby. Never doubt yourself . The 3.00 maybe nothing ,or maybe a small about . It wasn't the amount . It was the fact that she thought enough of the next person behind her not knowing who I was . The thought counted . I cried and praised God all the way home . I ask him to multiply her blessings . Sow seeds, and expect a great harvest. I have so many testimonies,but I gotta make room for others, but I wanna encourage somebody. Trust God , Always keep the faith . We are nothing without God . My walk with him is my life line now . It's so important . Our souls are important to him . Get a close and personal relationship with God . We leave him sometimes,but he never leave us . I know if he did it for me he will do it for you . Keep reading his word . I'm my first testimony. I realize the only weapon I need is the "BIBLE" I wanna give a special thanks to this amazing WOG . I thank him for how he use you to reach so many lives through testimonies. And WOG ! You just don't know how millions are about to be delivered by this book of testimonies. Eyes haven't seen ,nor have ears heard how God is about to blow your mind to a different level . Get ready because you will see his Glory through others just from this book . And again ! Thank you for choosing me to tell the world about his goodness and how I was delivered from the penitentiary and the pits of hell!! I got happy all over again 😵 😵 😵

Yolanda Robinson

When Mommy Died

Growing up in a single parent home, my mom was the source for me and my five siblings. What ever we needed she was our number one contact. Our mother was a strong mother. She held it together for three girls and three boys and she did it with so much grace. Even though life happens from time to time, she didn't allow it to shake her faith. While we leaned on our mother, it was a very known fact that she leaned on God.

She was our provider when needed. She was our comforter when comfort was needed. She was our teacher, our leader, our nurturer, and her love for us was unconditionally.

When my mommy died,it pierce a hole in my heart that never could be filled. When my mommy died, it brought emotions of loneliness, hurt, and fear.

When my mommy died, I felt lost emotions that I really couldn't explained. Through all of the emotions, through all of the fear, I was reminded of the scripture my mom instilled in me at a very young age, Let not your heart be troubled: John 14 (KJV). My mom taught us that with God On our side there's no need to worry regardless of what we are faced with or encountered. She taught us that our Heavenly Father is always there He will never leave us or forsake us. When my mom died I cried unto Him, my Heavenly Father; to help me in me in my despair, to help me in my fear, to help me in my grief, to help

Minister Stephanie Halbert

me move from grief to healing. Now here I am today walking in my healing by the grace of God.

I WENT INTO A TAILSPIN

Just want to testify about how awesome God is!!! I was on my way from home, and about half way home traffic was stopped. I slowed down to let someone in, I was hit from behind by a person driving seventy five miles an hour, no braking at all! I went into a tailspin. I also hit another car, but God is so good, no one was seriously hurt. I had a mild concussion. I know it was God who covered me. Just want to say that's what happens when you're under the covering of his blood!!!

Love you Amy for what you do!

Earnestine Bowen- Davis

I WAS DIAGNOSED WITH OVARIAN CANCER

My name is Earnestine Jones and I would like to give all the honor and glory to my God for what he has brought me to and brought me through. Over a year ago, I was diagnosed with ovarian cancer. As I was sitting in my doctors office in Tupelo, Mississippi and he was explaining to me about the cancer he asked me three questions the first question was were you a sickly person my asked was no, the second question he asked do you have the family support, my answer was yes and the third question was do you have a spiritual support and my answer was yes, he said good because you're going to need it and I looked him dead in his eyes and said if my God brought me to this he will bring me through this, I am a living witness and I will tell anybody anywhere anytime to lean and depend on God no matter what you're going through and I can sit here today and look back over the struggle the last ten months that I went through and where I am today is because of God mercy. Every time Satan tried to come in and take over I will say get back Satan this is me my God and I. And I am a living witness what ever God said he would do you can take that to the bank and I would like to thank all of my families my friends and my church members Payne Chapel M B Church for stand by me On this journey.

Mrs. Earnestine Jones

HE DELIVERED ME FROM COCAINE

Ms. Takiana Bailey

God called me to preach when I was a senior in high school n I've been running every since!!I accepted the calling and was ready to do the Lord's work but satan pushed me back well I allowed him to n fail again !! But this time I'm ready but have a few areas I still need work in before I step out but I'm getting myself ready!!! But in the meantime wen I first got called I was scared and was young and wanted to live life !!! But took a WRONG turn that result in homosexual, drug addiction, sex, alcohol, prostitution,and a thief! But GOD!!!!

I prayed and asked him to deliver me for this certain drug I wanted him to take the taste out of my mouth and he did just that delivered me from cocaine n I can't thank him enough !!! I'm not where I want to be but I'm working towards it !!

Takiana Bailey

Minister Lashanna Guines

THE CANCER HAD SPREAD
MORE THAN THEY THOUGHT

On September 8, 2021 I went to the doctor with horrible pelvic pain the doctor did my exam and ultrasound they seen that my uterus was enlarged way passed the normal size and they also seen tumors as well so they did a biopsy and sent it to the lab and they came back cancerous but he cancer had spread more than they thought would result in surgery. So I went home and I prayed and rubbed my self down with blessed on every day until I went back for my follow up On September 13th Which was the date that we would discuss surgery and set a date but when I went back for my follow up they did another ultrasound before the doctor came in I could hear him outside the door asking the nurse did she really do my ultrasound she said yes as he enters the room he said Ms. Guines I have great news I don't know what happened but you won't need surgery because the tumors are gone and your uterus has gone back down to it's normal size I believe in prayer and I thank God for healing me.!!!

Lashanna Guines

THROUGH MORE THAN 14 HEART BATTERY REPLACEMENTS

Hey Amy, hope this is what you want... trying to decide what testimony to share of God's greatness is difficult. But I will share this one:

At the age of 14 I was diagnosed with an irregular heart beat and required having a pacemaker implanted. Through more than 14 battery replacements , I never gave up hope that one day I wouldn't need a pacemaker because I would be healed. There were some ups and downs but I was consistent in my belief that one day I would be healed. I remember in high school I wanted to participate in sports. I asked my father if I could, I'll never forget what he said. He asked "do you believe that you can" my answer was always yes. At the beginning of 2021 I was at my cardiologist preparing for another battery replacement when the doctor came in and said "you don't need a pacemaker anymore your heart is healed!!!

As I was driving home I cried the entire trip because what I had been praying for and hoping for had finally manifested. Whatever you are asking God for, don't stop praying don't stop believing because He will answer you prayer. Amen

MS. ZATE MCGEE

THAT SMALL VOICE SAID,
"SPEAK TO THE WIND"

As I look back spiritually God has always dealt with me on faith!! I'm talking about "right now "faith!! One lesson in particular is what I call "Speak to the wind "faith! I ask my boys to set the things that was on the garbage pile on fire. They did. After while I check on it, it had gotten out of control! My youngest son Dewayne was up the hill. I called him to help me put the fire out!

After a hectic time, we finally got the fire out! Bye this time my Sister Thelma came to visit so we went into the house chatting. After she left, I heard a small voice say "Go check and see if it'll still out." I kept doing what I was doing, thinking okay I'm gonna check. Then I heard the same small voice "Go check on the fire!" This time I went outside the wind was blowing now the fire had blaze back up only it was towards the woods, the dry pine needles was burning!! My Son had left I was alone! I turned on the water hose fill up a gallon bucket ran to the wooded area dash the water on the fire it went out. Then the wind blew it ignited again! After two of three attempts running back to the water hose (too short to reach the area) I was exhausted!! Praying and crying out to God to help me before it catches the trees and all on fire. That small voice said "speak to the wind and say peace be still! You have the same power as I have!! I didn't hesitate "Peace Be Still! I Shouted!! And to my amazement I declare it actually STOP blowing!!! I mean calm! So, through that I've learned that the same power that Jesus has, He through the Holy Ghost has given us!!

Pastor Martha Williams

I HAD NO BLOOD IN MY BODY

Let me tell you about the God that I serve.. I often think about when God asked the devil had he considered His servant Job. Well I feel like God asked him if he considered His servant Joyce! Glory to God for His love for little me. I was diagnosed with breast cancer in November of 2018. I had a lumpectomy in December. After returning to work, I had to miss nights, leave early, or just struggle through it. I went to the doctor or the hospital seems like weekly. My left side gave out, I hurted day in and day out. Finally, I refused to go back to the doctor or hospital and prayed that I would just sleep away. One day I had laid on the sofa for over 12 hours and my husband and son came home. They begged me to go to the hospital. I refused but my son picked me up and carried me to the car. They wanted to go to Tupelo but I cried so we went to Amory. When I got there, they ran tests and told me that I had no blood in my body, so I was given 3 units that night and admitted. I was there for 3 days and thought I was getting better, but then I was told that I had to be transferred to Tupelo. I cried (even though I worked there). I tried to go by car but was told that I was a high risk and had to go by ambulance. When I got there, I was told that I had leukemia in November of 2019. Lord when I say that I went through so much, hospitalized 3 weeks out of a month for chemotherapy until August (I think). Then had to go in for blood clots in my lungs and right leg. Then became septic while in the hospital and had to be put on medication to keep a blood pressure. Even told my family last year that I was not going to make it. Well God knew the plans that He has for me and glory to God I'm still here. My beautiful queens, don't let nobody tell you that you are out or the game is over because God has the final say. I thank God for my journey and I refuse to give up now. I had a stem cell transplant March 10th of this year and I currently have to travel to Jackson every other week, but God is with me every step of the way. Is it easy, no ma'am but God promised to never leave nor forsake me. Glory!!!!! I haven't been allowed to ring the bell for breast cancer being gone, but I rang my bell because God got whatever it is. I'm prepared but not ready to leave this mean and cruel world. I could go on forever but I pray that you each just hold on a little while longer.

I made it through!

Mrs. Joyce Johnson

UPDATE......I've started back having problems with my left side. But God keeps on blessing me. Yes, My God has truly been blessing me. My husband had a bad car accident, therefore I had to start back driving. Thank God that I haven't been having passing out spells. I still take precautions and try to limit exposure because I have just started to take my childhood vaccines. Some days I don't feel good or may even hurt, but I continue to praise God and say that I'm okay. What people don't understand about my answer is that I have a relationship with my Father, so when this world can no longer provide me a place, I have a place not made by hands.

I CAN'T DO THIS AGAIN; I'M ABOUT TO GIVE UP GOD!

Call Me Hannah- A Prayer of Restoration Answered
  By: Amanda N. Ewing

Reverence to my Lord and Master, first and foremost, as I give Him glory, through an abridged testimony of how He saw fit to bless my husband and I with a family of our own.

I often tell people to just call me Hannah. Many times, I found myself in a "drunken" prayer like her. I could relate to her- for I longed and prayed for a child just as she did. My husband, Jay, and I tried for many years to conceive. Sometimes we felt hopeless and exhausted. I exercised, took vitamins, advised with doctors, as my husband did likewise and changed other habits into healthier choices. After a few years went by, we finally saw a PLUS sign! We were beyond happy. Our baby was on the way! And a BOY he was!!! Our sweet Joseph Dean Ewing was growing inside of me. However, 9 months later, our hearts would become empty as Joseph was born still on March 10, 2014. Burying a child was the hardest thing we ever had to do. Deep sadness, loneliness, disgust, anxiety, blame, guilt, and anger found me. My grief was nearly inconsolable. Yet, somehow this loss made my spiritual relationship closer with God. (Just call me Hannah.) "Lord, this could never happen again! I'll die; I wouldn't make it through this again!" God quickly strengthened me and restored my faith!

Not giving up whatsoever, we quickly went back to work on our road to parenthood. Years went by of praying, fasting, bible study, learning of God, missionary work, deep spiritual 1:1 sessions with God at 100% commitment. Lo and behold, here comes loss number two. The doctor said, "Mrs. Ewing, there will not be a baby this time either; We don't have any answers; Your test results are normal; You will have to travel to see a specialist next time." On my couch, while enduring the process of miscarriage, I looked to God and I said," Didn't I tell you I can't handle this again?" (Just call me Hannah.)

Even after a prophetic message was given to me that I'd never lose another child, which was a test of my faith, here I am suffering and in pain physically and emotionally once again. "I can't do this again; I'm about to give up, God!" Then, God's grace and strength came and words of faith that were not of my own! NEVER GIVE UP! FAITH WITH-OUT WORKS IS DEAD! If i never have my own child, it sure won't be because I didn't try! If I have to lose 10 to get 1, I'm ready, Lord, to take this journey! I will have faith and trust in Jesus' name! Scripture came to mind [GOD WILL GIVE YOU THE DESIRES OF YOUR HEART!] Surrender, surrender! I will work my faith and God will see my sincerity! (Just call me Hannah). But this time, He is my pilot and I'm just a rider.

Check this: Just a few months later, PLUS comes again and we were so nervous, but we prayed to God like never before! LORD, WHICH DOCTOR SHOULD I USE? God led me and almost immedi-ately I was on the phone with Dr. James Holzhauer's office. This doctor was Godsent. He found out my diagnosis almost immediately while all along telling me, "I don't wear my faith on my sleeves, but I am a firm believer!" This doctor had just as much faith as I that this pregnancy and those to follow would be successful, and he was right! Glory hallelujah! Insurance paid over $7,000 a month on my medicines, which left me paying less than $200 a month! Everyone we knew was praying for us and our success. On December 19, 2016 our healthy baby boy, Jaycob SAMUEL Ewing, was born, and he was absolutely gorgeous and perfect. Oh God thank You! You truly blessed us!

> Looking back now in 2021, I can remember praying for restoration then. "Restore me, Oh God!" -praying hard and sincere just as Hannah. "What I lost, Lord, restore! Fill this empty heart! Jay and I have lost two babies to Heaven's gain over the years....but, as I look at my babies right at this moment, I realize He did just that. He restored us our losses. Not only do we have Jaycob SAMUEL, but we have a daughter as well, Cobie Christina, who was born December 14, 2020.

> We realize now, that our losses were just tests of our faith, and by God's mercy, we passed! I am grateful for Hannah, Samuel, Eli, Job, and all the biblical testimonies. We are all walking testaments today. Hallelujah for persistence through faith! Hallelujah for our God who answers prayers! When you see me praising and praying, just call me Hannah, and I will tell you, I KNOW you can get a prayer through.

I THOUGHT I WAS GOING TO SUCCEED IN KILLING MYSELF

Evangelist Shalaura McKinney

My testimony,

I honor God who is the head of my life my rock my fortress my refuge and my hiding place. As a child I was never wanted or desired from birth but I felt tolerated by people but God still let me LIVE! I was molested, sexually assaulted, ridicule, denounced, back-stabbed, lied on and persecuted. I was traumatized. I tried to commit suicide several times I hated myself In September 2018 I thought I was gonna succeed in killing myself I had severe depression and anxiety life had took a lot from me and I was tired even though I smiled on the outside but feeling broken on the inside. I was angry bitter and hurt. I had been married three times and every experience with my husband was horrible. I often wondered who would want me because I had three husband. Two babies and two baby daddies. In July 2020 I was diagnosed with covid my kidneys shut down and I couldn't breathe or walk. But by the grace of God I survived. I didn't believe I would die but i felt so lifeless. In Sept 2020 I was domestically assaulted I had to get eighteen stitches in my arm. The devil had me thinking I would never use my arm again. But God used my arm to save my life A shield" to cover my heart. My lord God he did again He saved me. In 2021 the lord has broken me down and now HE is rebuilding me back gracefully to be used by him to win souls. I am grateful to be alive able to worship him in spirit and in truth. To God be the Glory for my journey and testimony.

Another Testimony to add:

I had a house fire in May 2021. We lost EVERYTHING!! I stayed with family members and even stayed in my truck and hotels for few months as a single mother it was so hard but God has blessed me and my children with our own place starting over with new mindset

FAITH IS THE EVIDENCE OF A STRESS-FREE LIFE

Faith is evidenced by a stress-free life that has been completely submitted to God's care and control. Whether or not God grants my request, I am content in knowing that He knows what is best for me. As I lay my life (and faith) on the altar each day, I am confident that my Creator is ever present to provide for my needs and enable me to meet all challenges that I may encounter. When the world frets, I rejoice.

Ancient Israel frequently forgot the God who delivered them from bondage and performed countless miracles to demonstrate His love for them. May we be forever grateful to Him for His loving kindness to us as well! He cares so much for us that He made plans for our salvation before we were born. Our daily experiences with Him as our Lord should reinforce our faith in Him. God, the True Miracle Worker, has never failed or forsaken His children, and He never will.

Minister Pearlie Westbrooks

I SENTENCE YOU TO 20 YEARS

I sentence you to 20 years, 15 suspended, 5 to serve. Ms. Yolanda, I don't know you, but if you decide you want to party one last time, I will give you those 15 back plus 25."

These are the words that were spoken to me by the white-haired judge my lawyer and I stood in front of on October 2, 2018. I know what some of you are thinking, 5 years isn't much, which in the state of Mississippi having a violent crime says you have to serve 50% of your time. So it was 2 ½ years that I had to serve. Now I know you feel that 2 ½ years isn't much, but I can promise you that one day in the custody of MDOC is too long to be away from your family.

Hearing those words broke my heart, considering the fact that I had been almost 2 years drug-free, and working 2 jobs to get back on my feet and get my children back.

Even though I was heartbroken, I immediately knew God was sending me

Ms. Yolanda Wofford

on a mission. Truth be told, He had been preparing me for this part of my journey long before I had obtained this charge of aggravated DUI.

For years I had a pill addiction. It all started out with me having a headache. All it took for me to get addicted was for someone to offer me half of Lortab. After that 1st taste, It not only took away my headache, it took away my emotional and mental pain for the moment. Or so I thought.

At the time I was a full-time college student, worked a full-time job, and most importantly a full-time Mother. Over the years my addiction got worse. It caused me much loss such as cars, jobs, and even some relationships. Eventually, I moved back home with my Mom and had to drop out of school. I also sent my 2 girls away to Georgia to live with their Dad.

After being addicted to pills for so long, eventually, it led to me using other drugs when I did not have pills. I tried powder cocaine, heroin, and eventually ice/meth. That took me to a place mentally and physically, that was so scary. I lived in another dimension with evil that I could see and feel so close.

Eventually, I became so spiritually and physically destitute that I only had 2 choices, die or cry out to God. It is safe for you to assume that I chose the latter of the two. On April 3, 2017, I checked myself into the Pines and Cady Hill Rehabilitation center in Columbus, MS. When I arrived the receptionist said to me, you are not gonna want to leave when it's time for you to go.

I thought to myself, she must be crazy. Needless to say, the longest one is supposed to stay is 90 days, I left in 93.

The day I fell down on my knees and cried to the Lord to help me I told Him Lord, I'm scared, I don't want to be sick, or go through withdrawals but I don't know what else to do. At that moment He came and met me where I was, down in the trenches, at the bottom of the barrel.

I was dirty, broke, busted, and very disgusted. I took one step and He took 1,000 for me. While I was in detox, I did not get sick nor did I have horrible withdrawals.

You don't have to get yourself together before you go to God, in fact, you can't, it's impossible. No one can get themselves together, if we could there would be no need for God.

Today I have been home from prison for 6 months. I have been employed at Toyota for 5 months and blessed with a new car for 3 months. Oh, yea and my girls are currently back in Mississippi with me.

Stay tuned...

THINGS I NEED ARE COMING TO ME

My testimony is of faith, patience, and season I arrived in this place(spiritual place in GOD) and have learned to lean and depend on GOD. I lived for years worrying about the how the when's and the where's and toiling night and day to make things happen.

Pastor Carl Weston

All of a sudden things changed. I begin to seek HIM 1st and......and HIS righteousness then everything came back not my life. It's so amazing I'm at a point that I don't ask for anything. Things I need are coming to me. If it doesn't come then my father must think I don't need it. I take not what HE sends. Here is the short version of my testimony. Recently I was working at a barbershop. So while I'm out and about throughout the city I would pass out my business cards. One day I passed one out and ended up meeting a man who owned a large building. He had a salon inside, a coffee bar, car detailing shop, and a barbershop but no barber ◇

He said I need you and all this is yours do what ever you want to do with it. Let's get that money!!! ◇◇◇◇◇◇

Needless to say!! I'm in a new location

Praise the Lord and to GOD be the glory

Ms. April Bowens-Hines

I BECAME STRESSED AND DEPRESSED WEIGHING 596 POUNDS

Giving reverence to an Awesome God whom I serve. Nothing is possible without him. I'm very grateful for this opportunity to share my testimony. Through-out my whole life, I have struggled with many things. Weight loss was the biggest part of my struggle. In 2015 my life changed drastically. The devil knocked on my door and I let him in. I became stressed and depressed weighing 596 lbs. At one point I did not want to live. For several months I stayed closed up in my dark bedroom. I did not hardly have mobility. I was so overweight that my legs will give out. I was not able to visit family and friends like I use to. I often felt that I was failing as a mother and as a wife. My children suffered because I was not able to attend different school functions they were involved in or do fun things with them. My late husband, Lord rest his soul, would get up every morning at 4:30am to help me bathe and get dress. He got the girls up for school and made sure they were straight.He would fix breakfast and made sure I had everything I needed right there in my reach before leaving for work. He did all of that every morning for several months and had to be at work at 7:00am.

On September 13, I was tired of living that way. I called a social worker at Baptist Memorial Hospital in Columbus asking for help. I was in a dark place and did not see a light at the end of the tunnel. I wanted to become the mother and wife I was at the beginning. I was admitted into the hospital. My social worker stated that I could not return home in the condition I was in. I was not able to stand, walk, or even take care of myself because of the excessive amount of weight I was carrying. She began calling around to different facilities to see will they take me as a in-house patient. Of course, I wanted to be close to home, but unfortunately several facilities would not take me. They had weight limitations. They could not accommodate me and my needs. She finally found a nursing home in Yazoo City that would take me. I left for Yazoo City on September 15, 2015. I went wanting to loose weight, walk again, and become a better me. Unfortunately, it did not work out that way. Even though the people were nice and showed me love, I was home sick & wanting to go home to my babies. I could not focus and did not progress in physical therapy because my mind was on home. When my family came to visit, I could see the hurt in my babies eyes and they cried every time before leaving me. I stayed there from September 2015 to February of 2017. In January of 2017 I spoke to social worker at the facility and she introduced me to the Medicaid Wavier Program. A program I have never heard of. The program provides the services I needed. After returning home, I had home health nurses to come and help with what I needed. Physical therapist came in my home to help me exercise and build my strength up to walk again.

In July 2019, my husband had a stroke(first of many) on his job. He was not able to return to work. For several months there were no income coming in, But GOD......We did not lack of anything. Lights never turned off, no eviction notices,no repro of our vehicles and we never went hungry. I thank God because he never left me nor forsaken me. I knew I had to do something. So I became determined.I had a husband and two babies that needed me. Depression tried to return in my life but GOD intervened. My doctor put me on a medication for depression. The medication also helped with my weight loss. Often times people would tell me I have lost weight and my reply would be "where" & laugher. I even considered weight loss surgery. After realizing that I was losing weight for real. I wanted to continue doing what I was doing. With the help of GOD, supportive family & friends I was able to take care of my husband ,be a great wife and mother again. My husband passed on October 18, 2020 and from that moment I decided to live & NOT die..... He was full of life. So,I am living and going on with my life as he would want me to. I will not give up because GOD has not given up on me. He kept me back then and he's keeping me now. I was broken and torn at a place of no return BUT GOD..............

I HAD A LOT OF DARK NIGHTS
BUT GOD PULLED ME OUT

Mrs. Rebecca Lao

Hello Amy, this is my testimony: When I had covid back last November; I didn't know what to think or what was gonna to happen. Sitting in one room for two weeks not knowing if I was gonna to live or die. So many thoughts came into my mind but I knew God was right there with me .God kept telling me to hold on to my faith God would tell me "Where is your faith"? He would tell me don't let fear take over your life. He told me that I must fight. I had alot of dark nights but God pulled me out. I must tell everyone that going through something just put everything in God's hands He will work it out. It may not seem like He's hearing you but He is right there by your side. Don't give up, keep pushing!! Hold on to your faith!! You will make it because I am living witness; God will provide your every needs. Thank God for not giving up on little ole me!!!

Rebecca Lao

Minister Louann Edwards-Walker

I WAS BLIND...BUT NOW I SEE

FAITH ISN'T A FEELING.
IT'S A CHOICE TO TRUST GOD EVEN WHEN
THE ROAD AHEAD SEEMS UNCERTAIN.

One day

the Doctor told me that I was diabetic and that it was affecting my eyes. My eyes had started to bleed in the back. So they began to give me shots in my eyes. And soon after that I had to undergo lots of laser surgeries. And then, it's like I just went blind.

I was already praying, and I didn't get weary because I told God that I wanted to see. Matthew 15:28, Jesus answered and said, "O woman, great is your faith; be it unto thee even as you will!

BUT it seemed like the more I prayed, the more problems would come. Sometimes I would wake up and see the blood in my eye. I just wanted the Lord to heal me right away. It didn't happen right away, I was going back again and again getting shots and lasers in my eyes.

AND one night my husband was reading the Bible to me, I looked at him and I said, "I can see you!" So it started a little at a time until I could see again.

THE blind men in Matthew 9:27-30; They followed Jesus crying, and saying,, "Thou Son of David have mercy on us (Lou). 28. When He was come into the house the blind men came to Him; and Jesus said unto them, Believe you that I am able to do this? They said unto him, Yes Lord. 29. The He touched their eyes saying, "According to your faith be it unto you. 30. And their eyes were opened.

I thank You Lord Jesus for healing y eyes! I know without a shadow of doubt He healed me, but I had to go through somethings to get there. 2 Corinthians 5:7 For we walk by faith, not by sight.

In my closing, Jude 1:20 But ye, beloved building up yourselves on your meat holy faith, praying in the Holy Ghost. Revelation 13:10 Here is the patience and the faith of the Saints.

-Minister Lou Ann Walker

TWICE I HAD POSITIVE BIOPSIES

He's an
Awesome God

Minister Mary C. Deanes

God has been and still is merciful to me. I will forever praise Him for His love and mercy. Twice I have been told that your biopsies are positive. Twice God came to my rescue. I'm so blessed in many ways because now I'm cancer free, my family was there for me and my insurances had covered my bills.

Most of all God has been faithful.

Yesterday I took another mammogram and the tech came back smiling and said "Ms. Deanes, You are free to go. Everything looks good you you are free to go." God is so so amazing.

I CAN FINALLY SEE

My physical sight left

But my SPIRITUAL sight became clear

Ms. Tawana Deanes

March 23, 2009, I got sick. I didn't realize what was going on with me. I was experiencing HEAT. My head felt hot on the inside. Prior to this, I had been dealing with sinus trouble, but I would not go to the Doctor no matter how my mom and family continued to tell me to go. I treated myself with over-the-counter medicines. That was only temporary. But that night, it all came down on me. The ambulance had to be called, I could remember my babies crying and screaming for me as they put me in the back of the ambulance. I was rushed to West Point to be told that I had an aneurysm, and they immediately rushed me to Tupelo, MS. After X-rays and MRI they discovered that I had not had an aneurysm, but I had a large tumor sitting behind my eye. A team of doctors and surgeons met to see what was best... But My family met to pray for me. The doctor did say that once the surgery was done, which was needed immediately it would be a possibility that I would lose my eyesight. The surgery was a success, they were able to get most of the tumor, that which was left..I had to get radiation done to shrink it. I stayed in the hospital in ICU for at least one month and then just in a step down room for about two months... My parents stayed with me every night. I got better, went through physical therapy and got out. I was just going back and forth for radiation to shrink the rest of the tumor. Standing in the flower bed one afternoon with my mom and sister and there it came Cerebellum Strokes, they came and I was rushed back to the hospital, this time my eyesight was taken. I was back in the hospital for about a month.

It took me a minute to realize how blessed I was but I did. It took my eyesight, but it could have been my life. It took my physical eyes to leave for me to see how Good God is. My physical sight left but my spiritual eyes were opened wide.

So I just look at it like this, I CAN FINALLY SEE!

QUICK SUBMIT AND COMMIT

Ms. Renata Roberts

Title: Quick Submit and Commit
Testimony: My daughter and I were going through a rough patch in life. I was working but I was barely making ends meet with all the demands on my life. My daughter never knew, but things were real rough. I remember going to the store one day and as I paid for the few things I had, I began to get frustrated and stress out. Prices were rising, but my income was not. I was being faithful in spending time with the Lord and giving (of my time and

income). It just seemed like so much. I started questioning how I would get groceries for the next week because I spent what I had this week and my next pay wasn't for another two weeks. Besides, the situation was going to be the same. I'm having an internal complaining session as I walk out the store and all of a sudden, I decided that my whole mood needed to change. I simply thanked God for what I had, told Him I trusted Him, and decided at that moment I was going to depend on Him instead of complaining to Him. Again, this is all internal but I'm quite sure it all could be read on my face! Ha-haha! By the time I got to the car, my phone rang. I answered it. It was my Pastor at the time calling to tell me that one of his son's shot a buck (that's a deer for those that don't know) and they wanted to give it to me. All I had to do was get it processed (cut and packaged into the meats of my choice) and give the son a steak from it. *Sooooo, you are just gonna show out real quick huh, Lord?!* I quickly agreed and thanked them and set up a time to get things taken care of. As I hung up, all I could do was thank God for not only providing, but over-providing! Here I was about to stress about just the next week and He provided for several months. It was not until I submitted my will and committed my trust that He instantly showed out. While I do not expect Him to be a genie in a bottle ready for my next request, I do know all I need to do is submit and commit to Him and He got me in His timing! I'm so glad I did it quickly! This is just one of the many ways He provides according to dependence!
Renata Roberts

Man Will Give Up On You, BUT Not GOD!

My testimony: when I was a small child I was in and out of the hospital. I was so sick that I couldn't walk talk or eat. I was constantly having seizures. The doctor told my mom there was nothing else they could do for me and that I wasn't going to live. I remember my Mom, Dad and my Aunt Cora bringing me home from the hospital. My Aunt carrying me in her arms into the house. My mom told me I got up one day and started walking talking and eating and haven't had a seizure since. What I'm trying to say is man will give up on you, but not God. The Doctor said I wasn't going to live, but my God said different. My God said I have plans for you. My Aunt Cora used to tell everyone how blessed I was. She would always tell my testimony of how sick I was when I was a small child wherever we were. My Aunt always testified what God has done for me. God has been so good to me. I'm a wife and mother of four girls, one granddaughter and a grand baby on the way. God has been so good to me and I am tremendously blessed. God has brought me from such a long way and I am so thankful and grateful for what he has done for me. I'm blessed with great friends, family, kids, grand-kids and a wonderful husband. I can't think him enough for what he has done for me.

Nita Chander

The Devil Tried To Make Me Question God

Words of encouragement to you oh mighty women, remember you are fearfully and wonderfully made in the image of God, in fact, you are the apples of His eyes. Before He formed you in your mother's womb He knew you, before you were born He set you apart. He already knew beforehand the plans He had for you oh mighty women. Plans to prosper you and not to harm you, plans to give you hope and a future. A future full of His goodness and mercy, to live a life of His abundant favor. As you continue to seek after God and the things of God, no good thing will He withhold from you.

There may be days when your world seems as if it's turned upside down and everything around you is falling apart but remember God's word says that He will never leave your nor forsake you. When it seems as if you can't go any further and you're at the end of your rope, it is in those times when He will strengthen you. His word promises us that in our weakness, He is strong. His word says that in times of trouble we can call upon Him and He will answer us, even as we're calling upon Him. In fact, God loves you so much that He has given His angels charge to watch over us and to keep us from falling.

I can tell you firsthand, there will be days your faith will be tested. I often prayed for others to be healed and they received their healing. Then one day, I received a diagnosis of breast cancer. The devil tried to make me question God by telling me "see, you can pray for others to be healed but God didn't hear your prayer for yourself to be healed. I continued to believe in God's word for healing, I prayed and declared that by the strips of Jesus I was healed. I didn't receive my healing the way I thought, I had to have surgery to have the cancer removed but in all of that I never lost faith in God. His word helped me to go through twenty rounds of radiation treatment. The doctors keep telling me I would probably be very fatigue during the treatments but in faith I believed that I would not become fatigue, and not one day did I feel fatigue. It was my faith in God's word that brought me through the entire ordeal.

Each day I laid on that treatment table this scripture ringed loud in my spirit: Isaiah 43:2 "when you go through deep waters, I will be with you. When you go through rivers of difficulty, you will not drown. When you walk through the fire of oppression, you will not be burned up, the flames will not consumer you." Those words were word of assurance to me!

No matter where the trials of life may take you, who may come in and out of your life, or how lonely you may feel, know oh mighty women that you are NEVER alone.

Jessie Gillespie Walker

Minister Demonia Dee Dean

I ASKED GOD TO GIVE ME ENOUGH TIME TO GET MY ARRANGEMENTS TOGETHER

I decided 2015 would be the year that I would get myself together. I would start going to the gym again and watch what I eat. It looked like things were really working out for me, the weight was coming down and I was getting in shape.

I started being cold all the time, to the point that I would go and curl up on the floor of our hall bathroom by the heater to get warm.

It was time for my physical, I went to the doctor and the test results showed that I was anemic. My doctor asked me when I became anemic, and I smiled and said I was gonna ask you that question. They began a series of tests to try and find out where I was losing blood. I was so anemic, I had to begin taking blood transfusions. I had taken so many tests, I began to feel like we were never going to find out what was going on with me. There was one last test to take, a PET (Positron Emission Tomography) scan.

It revealed that there was a tumor the size of a great fruit on my liver and two spots on my lungs. My doctor told me that I had stage four liver cancer and it was terminal. When I heard those words all I wanted to do was to get some place so that I could call out to the Lord, talk to Him and be in His presence. I had to start taking chemotherapy, there were two different kinds. One was so strong I was only able to tolerate three of the six planned treatments. I asked God if He would please just give me enough time to get my affairs in order so my family wouldn't have to worry about things once I was gone. After I had completed doing everything I thought I needed to do I found myself having a conversation with God.

I thanked him for allowing me to have the time to get my affairs in order and then I said, " Lord I'm not ready to die but if this is your will for me, please help me to accept it". God said to me "I am going to perform a miraculous miracle in you but just know that you will not leave this earth until it is your time". God did not share with me what this miraculous miracle would be. I thought maybe it meant I would not suffer or be in great pain as I went through this experience to the end.

I continued my treatment and the tumor continued to shrink. My doctor could not believe what was happening. He had other doctors coming in and he would say "this is the patient I was telling you about".

My tumor continued to shrink until it had gotten down to the size of a dot. God is good and faithful, here it is six years later and now I am cancer free. I once had someone tell me that God does not perform miracles now like He used to. I told them yes, He does, you're looking at one.

Demonia (Dee) Dean

Author Frances Deanes
God is Bigger than Covid

HE ALWAYS GOT IN THE STORM WITH ME

I remember watching television during the heightened part of the PANDEMIC praying and asking God to cover me and my family. Seeing the count of people dying every day, knowing people in my family had underlying conditions, I was afraid. Then COVID hit my home, my husband, three other family members and me, BUT GOD! God shielded my daughters especially the one with underlying conditions. Even though it was rough God brought us through it and restored us again. So many storms I have been through, there's always been a BUT God. He always got in the storm with me . HALLELUJAH!!!!

AMY L. DEANES

BUILT FAITH

In a depression, because of the bad choices I made in my past, carried me down a road that looked hopeless. Not knowing who I could really trust or would not judge me had me thinking there was no way out! I had just enough word in me to know what Hebrews 9:14 says. "The Word of God will purge our conscience from dead works to serve the living God. And I had done things that was not pleasing to God because I was ignorant and in unbelief to His saying in 1 Timothy 1:13, knowing this helped to believe that God would help me in this situation and that I could face this insurmountable problem head on!

So that's what I did, I faced the past head on and in doing so it helped me to build my faith in God. I came to know and understand that He is a forgiving God, and my sins are already paid for.

Minister Lucy Davis

Minister Amy Deanes
Owner of Superior Publishing LLC
Cedar Bluff, MS

I would like to take this opportunity to thank each writer for their testimony. I appreciate you for taking the time out of your busy schedule and seeing about the assignment that God had given me. God had already ordained you for this. I just want to say thanks for help making it come together. I pray for God to bless each person individually and also collectively. I give God Glory for what He will do in the days, months and years to come in the lives of those that read this book and increase their faith.

I SPEAK BLESSINGS
I speak blessings over every participant, that this is just the beginning
of Great Things to come.

I speak a clean bill of health over every participant! I speak freedom in the heart and mind that You may go forth with no hesitation!

I speak prosperity that it begins in your mind that your mind may transform first and then your accounts become filled, IN JESUS NAME .

I speak deliverance from any demonic attack, stronghold, or spell that has you bound in the might name of JESUS.

I pray that the HOLY SPIRIT push you into the very place that you need to be without delay!!

I speak abundance in every area of your life that you lack nothing! Even before you open your mouth, God provides.